A special gift for

_____

from,

_____

date

_____

With love and admiration
for my dear sisters,
Nancy Gordon and Becky Cobb,
both great assets
to their workplaces and to me!

Other great books that
take a little look
at the big things of life

Life's Too Short to Leave Kite Flying to Kids
—for Busy Grownups

Life's Too Short to Look for Missing Socks
—for Moms

Life's Too Short to Give Up Slumber Parties
—for Girlfriends

Available where good books are sold.

A Little Look at the Big Things of Life

Life's Too Short

to YELL at Your Computer

HOWARD
PUBLISHING CO.

for the Workplace

Judy Gordon

Our purpose at Howard Publishing is to:
• *Increase faith* in the hearts of growing Christians
• *Inspire holiness* in the lives of believers
• *Instill hope* in the hearts of struggling people everywhere
Because He's coming again!

Life's Too Short to Yell at Your Computer © 2005 by Howard Publishing Co., Inc.
All rights reserved. Printed in China
Published by Howard Publishing Co., Inc.
3117 North 7th Street, West Monroe, LA 71291-2227
www.howardpublishing.com

05 06 07 08 09 10 11 12 13 14   10 9 8 7 6 5 4 3 2 1

Edited by Between the Lines and Chrys Howard
Cover design by LinDee Loveland
Interior design by Stephanie D. Walker and Tennille Paden
Illustrations by Cindy Sartain

ISBN: 1-58229-420-8

Contents

Chapter
One

Enjoyment

Life's
Too Short
to simply *settle*.

Life's
Too Short
to complain
about *overtime.*

enjoyment

Don't you love being around people who love their jobs? They walk with a bounce, speak with enthusiasm, and smile a lot. Such people can scarcely contain their enthusiasm regarding whatever projects they are working on. They embrace both the joys and the challenges.

One of their most noticeable attributes is how sincerely they enjoy the people they work with. They also know how to listen and when to be decisive. They exude confidence but not arrogance, and others benefit just by being around them.

What's their secret? While many elements play a role, two are key: optimism and balance. These people show optimism in how they think of themselves and others. They show balance by loving what they do but not being obsessed by it. They don't dread Monday, but they still look forward to the weekend. Work isn't their life; they work and live life fully.

I commend enjoyment, for there is nothing better for people under the sun than to eat, and drink, and enjoy themselves, for this will go with them in their toil through the days of life that God gives them under the sun.

ECCLESIASTES 8:15
NRSV

Life's
Too Short

to save your

best

for last.

Life's
Too Short
to bring work home.

Is there someone you admire
in your workplace
who portrays positive attitudes
and a zest for work and life?
Consider asking that person to be your mentor.

Chapter Two

Courtesy

to wait for a coworker to start the coffee.

Life's
Too Short

Life's
Too Short

to think
good manners
don't apply

at work.

courtesy

In any job setting, it doesn't take long to acquire a positive or negative reputation for courtesy. Kelly is known for being late. Sandy often brings homemade cookies or other treats for staff meetings. Everyone knows when Pete uses the copier because of all the papers and clutter he leaves behind. Chris often interrupts.

How quickly our behavior patterns are etched in the thoughts of our coworkers. Regardless of a person's strengths in other areas, courtesy in the workplace—or the lack of it—sets a first impression that can be as permanent as a handprint in concrete.

Courtesy counts. It shows respect for others. A friendly disposition makes for smooth work relationships. Colleagues won't remember every word you've said, but they will recall your pleasant demeanor and gracious attitude.

Make sure that nobody
pays back wrong for wrong,
but always try to be kind
to each other
and to everyone else.

1 THESSALONIANS 5:15

Life's
Too Short

to expect your workplace to revolve around **you.**

Life's
Too Short

to say,

"Fix it," and not say,

"Please."

You may be the most considerate person
in your workplace, or you may need
to improve your workplace manners.
Choose one thing to change,
and be consistent.
Then enjoy the difference courtesy makes.

Chapter
Three

Communication

Life's
Too Short

to think that **words** can never harm you or others.

speaks volumes.

body language

to forget that

Life's
Too Short

communication

Perhaps all of us can replay in our minds words that have impacted our lives forever. Too often it's the hurtful, negative comments that we so easily recall. Extreme statements laced with *always* and *never*. Fortunate and rare are those who, even years later, recall optimistic, constructive words instead of hurtful, destructive ones that echo painfully in their memories.

Words wield power, and we need much wisdom as we both speak and listen. Do your words bring hope or harm? Are you obviously distracted and uninterested, or do you listen with rapt attention when others speak to you?

Good communication is vital in all realms of life, and the workplace is no exception. The words we speak and the way we listen reflect what lies within us and will often determine success on the job—for ourselves and even for others.

What kind of communicator are you?

My mouth would encourage you;
comfort from my lips
would bring you relief.

JOB 16:5

Life's
Too Short

to never master the art of "zipping it."

Life's
Too Short

to be part of the problem, not the solution.

If a friend at work talks
negatively about someone,
gently say something positive in response.
Your comment can counteract that harm
and turn the conversation around.

Chapter
Four

Fun

Life's
Too Short

to decide *hula-hoops* have no place at work.

Life's
Too Short
to wear
a suit
on casual day.

fun

The employees talked about it for weeks after the company picnic. And they couldn't talk about it without laughing all over again. The event? Their supervisors raced each other on tiny red tricycles.

Surveys have shown that a fun work environment brings higher productivity. Fun dissolves stress and makes employees happier. And happy employees do better work. In a fun workplace, employees are more likely to greet customers with a smile and maintain a friendly attitude. An upbeat environment is contagious, affecting both workers and clients positively.

Opportunities for fun abound. How about a yearly talent show in which each department puts on a humorous skit? Or have various groups sing carols at the Christmas party with new lyrics appropriate to the business. And don't forget to look for the many daily opportunities to inject fun and joy into that place you call your second home.

A cheerful heart
is good medicine,
but a crushed spirit
dries up the bones.

PROVERBS 17:22

Life's
Too Short

to think
the
Workplace
is really only
for
work.

Life's
Too Short

to treat

your work friends
as mere
coworkers.

Find the perfect spot
to post appropriate cartoons and jokes,
and appoint someone to serve as the Laugh Master
to oversee and update the contributions.
Enjoy the shared laughter!

Chapter
Five

Attitude

Life's
Too Short

to forget
the Golden Rule.

you hear.

everything everything everything

everything everything everything

to believe

Life's
Too Short

attitude

A coworker gives a brusque answer, and you wonder what you did to deserve it. Probably nothing. So many things occur each workday that could cause you to take offense. Rather than doing that, consider trying another option: assume the best.

When someone doesn't return your smile, assume the best. When you wonder why the person next to you isn't responding to your jovial chatter, assume the best. And when your boss seems so preoccupied that you feel overlooked and underappreciated, assume the best.

Apply these possibilities to the above people. Maybe she just learned her mother has cancer. Perhaps he's worried about his marriage. Your boss might be preoccupied with a tough decision. And when you're having a rough day after a sleepless night of worrying, you'll appreciate it when your colleagues take the high road and assume the best about you.

Dear friends,
let us love one another,
for love comes from God.
Everyone who loves
has been born of God
and knows God.

1 JOHN 4:7

Life's
Too Short *to think you*
already know
the rest of the story.

Life's Too Short to worry that someone is talking about you.

The best solution for offsetting potentially hurtful
situations with coworkers is prayer.
When you pray for someone,
you're acting out God's equivalent
of "assuming the best."

Chapter Six

Encouragement

Life's
Too Short

to leave the smiley-face stickers to teachers.

to save flowers for special occasions.

Life's
Too Short

encouragement

Affirmation. Praise. Celebration. All are important factors to ensure a positive work environment. We need those notes that give us a written pat on the back. We appreciate the boost to our spirits a word of praise gives. We enjoy the warm feeling when we celebrate each other's successes.

If your workplace lacks in these areas, maybe you can do something to change that. It takes only one person to start a positive revolution. Don't just notice when people do things wrong. Notice what they do right. Say thank you for even the small things they do well. Pass on the compliments you hear others say about them. Write an anonymous note and stick it by the phone of a fellow employee who needs or deserves encouragement.

You might be surprised at how easy it is to improve the atmosphere of openness and appreciation where you work. Who knows, you might even find some of that appreciation and encouragement coming back to bless you.

Encourage one another
and build each other up,
just as in fact you are doing.

1 THESSALONIANS 5:11

Life's
Too Short

to skip the
"thank you."

Life's
Too Short

to think only
six-year-olds need
to hear, "Good job!"

Be specific and sincere in your praise.
Commend someone for that excellent presentation
or that calm response to an irate client.
Leave a note, a candy bar, or flower to say,
"Way to go!"

Chapter Seven

Atmosphere

Life's
Too Short
to have a
boring
screensaver

Life's
Too Short

to leave family pictures at home.

atmosphere

What do people see when they come into your workspace? Are their eyes drawn to photos of family and friends? Do they zero in on the kaleidoscope sitting on your desk? Or maybe it's your collection of polished agates in an abalone shell.

Since you spend almost a third of your time at work, add some pizzazz to make even the smallest of work stations a pleasant place. Surround yourself with favorite things, like some old Superman comic books or a jar full of antique buttons or marbles. Or cover an entire wall with your favorite Far Side cartoons. Post a map of the best hiking trails.

When your work spot is warm and inviting, it extends a welcome to others. And when it reflects your personality and interests, it also allows others to get to know more about you outside the job setting. So get creative and show your stuff!

Let the beauty of the L<small>ORD</small> our God be upon us, and establish the work of our hands for us.

PSALM 90:17
NKJV

Life's
Too Short

to use
plain
manila
folders.

to leave the Simon and Garfunkel CD in the car.

Life's
Too Short

Keep a candy jar on your desk
filled with seasonal treats.
It will welcome coworkers
or act as an icebreaker at a new job.

Chapter
Eight

Bad Days

computer.
at your

to yell

Life's
Too Short

Life's
Too Short

to expect
every day
to be
perfect.

bad days

Don't you hate those days when every little thing that can go wrong does? You wake up on the wrong side of the bed, fight traffic, drop your keys in a muddy gutter—and you haven't even made it to the office yet!

The downward spiral continues. A coworker offers a scowl rather than the usual smile, no one has made the coffee, and you're greeted with a disgruntled message on your voice mail. Now would probably be the perfect time to reach for a copy of the picture book *Alexander and the Terrible, Horrible, No Good, Very Bad Day* by Judith Viorst. Then even when your computer freezes for the umpteenth time and the person using the microwave before you doesn't clean up the chili overflow, you can remind yourself that you're having an Alexander day. And some days are just like that.

Satisfy us in the morning
with your unfailing love,
that we may sing for joy and
be glad all our days.

PSALM 90:14

Life's
Too Short

to assume everyone will like everything you do.

Life's
Too Short
not to

smile anyway.

One tip for eliminating a potential annoyance:
Discard every writing implement that doesn't work.
Then stock up on your favorite colors and brands,
and color your day happy.

Chapter
Nine

Faith

Life's
Too Short
to forget
that everyone
has another
life.

Life's
Too Short
to save
prayer
for meals and bedtime.

faith

Has this happened to you? Your phone rings, and you hear the tears in your coworker's voice: "Will you please pray for me? I'm waiting for the results of some medical tests, and I'm worried."

Your place of employment offers the perfect opportunity to demonstrate faith, even if you never say a word. Your godly actions and attitudes will reveal what's inside you. Someday you may even be asked, "Why are you always so upbeat and positive?" What a wonderful opportunity to explain that it's because of your personal faith in Jesus Christ. Don't be afraid to tell people at work that He makes all the difference in your life.

If you're a Christian, God has placed you where you work for a reason. Be His love in action. And when others are faced with a crisis, they'll know just where to turn.

Let your light shine before men,
that they may see your good deeds
and praise your Father in heaven.

MATTHEW 5:16

Life's
Too Short

to forget
who you
really
work for.

Life's
Too Short
to hide Jesus
in your heart.

Keep a daily calendar
on your desk
that features inspirational
quotes and scriptures.
Besides benefiting you,
those words could be just
what a coworker needs.